Must-Have Blender Cookbook for Everyone

The Most Delicious Recipes That You Can Prepare in Your Blender

BY: Valeria Ray

License Notes

Copyright © 2019 Valeria Ray All Rights Reserved

All rights to the content of this book are reserved by the Author without exception unless permission is given stating otherwise.

The Author have no claims as to the authenticity of the content and the Reader bears all responsibility and risk when following the content. The Author is not liable for any reparations, damages, accidents, injuries or other incidents occurring from the Reader following all or part of this publication.

A Special Reward for Purchasing My Book!

Thank you, cherished reader, for purchasing my book and taking the time to read it. As a special reward for your decision, I would like to offer a gift of free and discounted books directly to your inbox. All you need to do is fill in the box below with your email address and name to start getting amazing offers in the comfort of your own home. You will never miss an offer because a reminder will be sent to you. Never miss a deal and get great deals without having to leave the house! Subscribe now and start saving!

https://valeria-ray.gr8.com

Contents

Delicious Blender Recipes 7

(1) Acai and Raspberry Smoothie.. 8

(2) Banana Spinach Smoothie 10

(3) White Chocolate Mousse.. 12

(4) Blender Guacamole 14

(5) Hummus Dip... 16

(6) Banana Pancakes 18

(7) Blackberry Ice Cream 21

(8) Apple & Greens Juice 23

(9) Broccoli and Turnip Soup 25

(10) Creamy Carrot Juice 28

(11) Grapefruit Sorbet 30

(12) Blueberry & Grape Slush 32

(13) Greens Soup 34

(14) Grapefruit & Carrot Juice 37

(15) Creamy Tomato Soup 39

(16) Pineapple Ginger Juice 42

(17) Cherry Kiwi Ice Cream 44

(18) Peanut Cookies 46

(19) Baked Blueberry Pancake 49

(20) Kabocha Squash and Broccoli Soup 52

(21) Kabocha Chocolate Chip Muffins 55

(22) Ginger Spiced Soup 58

(23) White Chocolate Fudge 61

(24) Kale - Artichoke Dip 63

(25) Apple Whip 66

(26) Tahini Avocado Dip 68

(27) Strawberry Smoothie 70

(28) Grapefruit, Banana & Pomegranate Smoothie 72

(29) Blackberry Chocolate Blast 74

(30) Roasted Beet Dip 76

About the Author 79

Author's Afterthoughts 81

Delicious Blender Recipes

MMMMMMMMMMMMMMMMMMMMMMMMMMMMMMM

(1) Acai and Raspberry Smoothie

Acai berries are considered to have numerous health benefits. This delicious smoothie allows you to enjoy the benefits of both raspberries and Acai.

Makes: 2

Preparation Time: 5 minutes

List of Ingredients:

- ½ cup acai berries
- 1 cup Greek yogurt
- 1 tsp. vanilla paste
- 1 cup fresh strawberries, hulled and sliced
- Water to max line

MMMMMMMMMMMMMMMMMMMMMMMMMMMMMM

Instructions:

1. Place acai berries, strawberries and Greek yogurt in blender.

2. Add water to max line and process for 30 seconds.

3. Serve immediately.

(2) Banana Spinach Smoothie

Perfect smoothie, rich in fibers and can be served during breakfast.

Makes: 1

Preparation Time: 5 minutes

List of Ingredients:

- 1 medium ripe banana
- 2 cups spinach leaves chopped
- 1 Tbsp. flax seed
- Liquid to the max line (milk, water, coconut milk etc.)
- 1 ½ cups of vanilla Greek yogurt

MMMMMMMMMMMMMMMMMMMMMMMMMMMMMMM

Instructions:

1. Place banana, spinach, flax seeds and yogurt in blender.

2. Add enough liquid, by your choice to reach max line and process until smooth.

3. Serve immediately.

(3) White Chocolate Mousse

Fat mousse prepared in blender. Rich and decadent.

Makes: 2

Preparation Time: 5 minutes

List of Ingredients:

- ¼ cup melted chocolate
- 2 cups heavy whipping cream
- ½ tsp. Grapefruit extract

MMMMMMMMMMMMMMMMMMMMMMMMMMMMMMM

Instructions:

1. Place all ingredients into a blender.

2. Process until desired consistency is reached.

3. Chill before serving.

(4) Blender Guacamole

Everyone loves guacamole and is must have dip for each party. We bring you so fast and simple version, but also very delicious.

Makes: 2

Preparation Time: 5 minutes

List of Ingredients:

- ¾ cup tomatoes, chopped
- 2 Tbsp. lemon juice
- 2 avocados, peeled, pitted
- ½ cup cilantro, fresh
- ¼ cup onion, chopped

MMMMMMMMMMMMMMMMMMMMMMMMMMMMM

Instructions:

1. Place all ingredients in a blender.

2. Turn the machine and blend on low for 10 seconds increase the speed to medium and blend for 10 seconds. Stop the machine, scrape down the sides of bowl and process again for 10 seconds.

3. Serve after.

(5) Hummus Dip

This delicious dip can be enjoyed with veggie crudités or crackers.

Makes: 10

Preparation Time: 5 minutes

List of Ingredients:

- 3 cups chickpeas, cooked
- 2 garlic cloves, peeled
- 2 Tbsp. extra-virgin olive oil
- 1 tsp. cumin, ground
- ½ cup water
- ¼ cup lemon juice
- ¼ cup sesame seeds
- ½ Thai chili

MMMMMMMMMMMMMMMMMMMMMMMMMMMMMMM

Instructions:

1. Place all ingredients in a blender. Start blending on low.

2. Increase speed to high and process for 60 seconds or until desired consistency is reached.

3. Serve after.

(6) Banana Pancakes

These delicious pancakes are perfect for Sunday brunch.

Makes: 6

Preparation Time: 15 minutes

List of Ingredients:

- 3 eggs
- 3 Tbsp. melted butter
- 1 cup whole-wheat flour
- 1 ½ cups milk
- 1 cup all-purpose flour
- 2 tsp. baking powder
- ½ tsp. salt
- 2 Tbsp. honey
- 2 ripe bananas, sliced

MMMMMMMMMMMMMMMMMMMMMMMMMMMMMM

Instructions:

1. In a bowl combine the flours, salt and baking powder.

2. In a blender combine the milk, honey, melted butter and bananas. Process until smooth.

3. Fold the banana mix into the dry ingredients and continue stirring until smooth.

4. Let the batter rest for 10 minutes and preheat your pancake pan. Pour 1/3 cup batter in the pan and cook for about 4 minutes.

5. Repeat until all your batter has been used.

6. Serve with fresh fruits.

(7) Blackberry Ice Cream

Now you can easily create delicious ice cream at home using fresh fruit and your blender.

Makes: 6

Preparation Time: 5 minutes

List of Ingredients:

- 1lb. frozen blackberries
- 1 cup milk
- ½ tsp. vanilla paste
- ¾ cup sugar

MMMMMMMMMMMMMMMMMMMMMMMMMMMMMM

Instructions:

1. Process the blackberries, milk, vanilla and sugar for 40 seconds.

2. Chill additionally before serving.

(8) Apple & Greens Juice

Vegetable juices are often off to swallow. But this recipe aims to correct that by providing the perfect blend of vegetables and apples.

Makes: 3 ½ Cups

Preparation Time: 15 minutes

List of Ingredients:

- Water (1/2 cup)
- Cucumber (1 large, chopped)
- Celery (1 ½ Stalks quartered)
- Apples (2 large, seeded, quartered)
- Kale Leaves (2 Cups)
- Ginger (1-inch piece, peeled)

MMMMMMMMMMMMMMMMMMMMMMMMMMMMM

Instructions:

1. Pour all your ingredients into the Blender and secure the lid.

2. Slowly increase the speed while blending for 1 minute.

3. Use the tamper to push the ingredients down until desired consistency is reached.

4. Chill, serve and enjoy!

(9) Broccoli and Turnip Soup

This soup is rich, creamy and delicious.

Makes: 6

Preparation Time: 30 minutes

List of Ingredients:

- 1.5lb. broccoli
- 7oz. turnip, peeled and diced
- 2 cups chicken stock
- 3 Tbsp. ghee
- 1 onion, chopped
- 5oz. chorizo, chopped
- Salt – to taste

MMMMMMMMMMMMMMMMMMMMMMMMMMMMMM

Instructions:

1. Wash the broccoli and cut into small florets, set aside.

2. Melt 2 Tbsp. ghee in Dutch oven and add chopped onion, cook for 5 minutes. Stir in prepared broccoli and cook for 5-6 minutes, stirring.

3. Stir in chicken stock and cover with lid, cook for 10 minutes.

4. Meanwhile, melt the remaining ghee and cook chorizo with turnips for 8-10 minutes.

5. Transfer half of the chorizo mixture into soup, remove soup from the heat and allow to cool for 10 minutes. Transfer the soup into a blender and puree in batches if needed.

6. Season to taste, serve in small bowls and top with reserved chorizo mix.

(10) Creamy Carrot Juice

This recipe gives a rich blend of carrot. If you love creamy drinks you will love this!

Makes: 5 cups

Preparation Time: 11 minutes

List of Ingredients:

- Heavy Cream (2 cups)
- Carrots (12 oz., diced)
- Ice Cubes (2 Cups)

MMMMMMMMMMMMMMMMMMMMMMMMMMMMMM

Instructions:

1. Pour all your ingredients into the Blender and secure the lid.

2. Slowly increase the speed while blending for 45 seconds.

3. Serve and Enjoy!

(11) Grapefruit Sorbet

This delicious sorbet is just the right amount of sweet and sour.

Makes: 6

Preparation Time: 5 minutes

List of Ingredients:

- 4 ½ cups ice cubes, crushed
- 2 Tbsp. sugar
- 2 Grapefruits, segmented
- 1 Tbsp. grated Grapefruit zest
- 2 Tbsp. honey

MMMMMMMMMMMMMMMMMMMMMMMMMMMMMM

Instructions:

1. Place all ingredients in a blender. We suggest that you make the sorbet in batches.

2. Blend the ingredients for 30 seconds.

3. Serve immediately.

(12) Blueberry & Grape Slush

This is a wacky combination that provides a delicious sensation!

Makes: 2 ½ Cups

Preparation Time: 11 Minutes

List of Ingredients:

- Green Grapes (1 cup)
- Red Grapes (1 cup)
- Blueberries (1 cup, frozen)
- Ice Cubes (½ Cup)

MMMMMMMMMMMMMMMMMMMMMMMMMMMMMMM

Instructions:

1. Pour all your ingredients into the Blender and secure the lid.

2. Slowly increase the speed while blending for 45 seconds.

3. Serve and Enjoy!

(13) Greens Soup

This soup is the perfect kick you need to jump start your day.

Makes: 6

Preparation Time: 30 minutes

List of Ingredients:

- 14oz. broccoli, cut into florets
- 5oz. watercress
- 7oz. kale, thawed
- 4 cups chicken stock
- 1 cup coconut milk
- ¼ cup ghee
- Salt and pepper – to taste
- 1 onion, chopped
- 2 garlic cloves, crushed

MMMMMMMMMMMMMMMMMMMMMMMMMMMMMMM

Instructions:

1. Grease Dutch oven with ghee, place over medium-high heat and add onion and garlic. Cook until browned and stir broccoli florets. Cook for 5 minutes.

2. Add kale and water cress and cook for 2 minutes or until just wilted, pour in vegetable stock and bring to boil.

3. Cook until broccoli is crisp-tender and stir in the coconut milk.

4. Season with salt and pepper and remove from the heat. Allow cooling and puree the soup in blender until creamy. Serve immediately.

(14) Grapefruit & Carrot Juice

Refreshing Carrot Juice with a dash of grapefruit.

Makes: 2 ½ Cups

Preparation Time: 6 minutes

List of Ingredients:

- Water (1 Cup)
- Carrots (1 ½ Cup, diced)
- Grapefruit Juice (2 tsp., freshly squeezed)
- Ice Cubes (1 Cup)

MMMMMMMMMMMMMMMMMMMMMMMMMMMMMMM

Instructions:

1. Pour all your ingredients into the Blender and secure the lid.

2. Slowly increase the speed while blending for 1 minute.

3. Serve and Enjoy!

(15) Creamy Tomato Soup

If you love Italian cuisine you will greatly appreciate this soup.

Makes: 4

Preparation Time: 30 minutes

List of Ingredients:

- 28oz. tomatoes, peeled and pureed
- 1 cup heavy cream
- 1 onion, diced
- 1 tsp. fresh ground pepper
- 4 cups chicken stock
- ½ cup grated Parmesan
- 1 bunch celery, chopped
- ½ cup basil, chopped
- 1 Tbsp. olive oil
- Salt and pepper – to taste

MMMMMMMMMMMMMMMMMMMMMMMMMMMMMMM

Instructions:

1. Heat olive oil in large pot over medium-high heat, add onion, with celery and cook until tender.

2. Pour chicken stock and tomatoes in the pot, bring mixture to simmer and season with salt and pepper. Simmer for 30 minutes.

3. Turn off heat and allow the soup to cool down. Puree in blender in batches.

4. Stir in heavy cream, basil and Parmesan cheese.

5. Serve immediately.

(16) Pineapple Ginger Juice

This refreshing drink will transport you to the tropics.

Makes: 3 Cups

Preparation Time: 6 minutes

List of Ingredients:

- Pineapple Chunks (2 ½ Cups)
- Ginger (1-inch root, peeled, chopped)
- Ice Cubes (1 Cup)

MMMMMMMMMMMMMMMMMMMMMMMMMMMMMMM

Instructions:

1. Pour all your ingredients into the Blender and secure the lid.

2. Slowly increase the speed while blending for 1 minute.

3. Use the tamper to push the pine down until desired consistency is reached.

4. Serve and Enjoy!

(17) Cherry Kiwi Ice Cream

Combine sweet cherries with delicious kiwi to create a tropical explosion in your home blender.

Makes: 6

Preparation Time: 5 minutes

List of Ingredients:

- ½ lb. frozen kiwi
- ½ lb. frozen cherries
- 1 cup milk
- ½ tsp. vanilla paste
- ¾ cup sugar

MMMMMMMMMMMMMMMMMMMMMMMMMMMMMM

Instructions:

1. Process the cherries, kiwi, milk, vanilla and sugar for 40 seconds.

2. Chill additionally before serving.

(18) Peanut Cookies

Here is a quick and easy cookie recipe that you can prepare even if you do not have a mixer on hand.

Makes: 24 cookies

Preparation Time: 25 minutes

List of Ingredients:

- ½ cup sugar
- 1 egg
- ¾ cup whole-wheat flour
- ½ cup silvered peanuts
- ½ tsp. peanut extract
- ½ cup butter spread
- 1 Tbsp. milk
- ¼ tsp. baking soda
- 1 pinch salt

MMMMMMMMMMMMMMMMMMMMMMMMMMMMMM

Instructions:

1. Preheat oven to 350F and line baking sheet with baking paper.

2. In a blender combine the butter spread, egg, sugar, peanut extract and milk. Process until smooth.

3. Add the baking soda, peanuts and flours. Process for 15 seconds more or until blended thoroughly. Drop the cookie batter onto cookie sheet and bake for 15 minutes.

4. Remove from the oven and place aside to cool. Serve at room temperature.

(19) Baked Blueberry Pancake

Here is a simple pancake recipe that you can whip up easy with a blender then just toss it in the oven.

Makes: 4

Preparation Time: 30 minutes

List of Ingredients:

- 1 cup fresh blueberries, chopped
- 1 cup all-purpose flour
- 1 egg, whisked
- 1 ½ tsp. baking powder
- ¾ cup milk
- 3 Tbsp. honey
- 2 Tbsp. butter + some for the pan, melted

MMMMMMMMMMMMMMMMMMMMMMMMMMMMMM

Instructions:

1. Preheat oven to 350F and place 10-inch oven-proof skillet in the oven.

2. In a blender combine the egg, milk, melted butter and honey.

3. In a bowl combine the flour with baking powder. Fold in the liquid ingredients and stir until smooth. Remove the skillet from the oven and brush with melted butter.

4. Pour in the prepared batter and sprinkle with chopped blueberries. Bake the pancake for 25 minutes. Remove and place aside to cool. Slice and serve at room temperature.

(20) Kabocha Squash and Broccoli Soup

Super healthy and vibrant soup everyone will love.

Makes: 4

Preparation Time: 25 minutes

List of Ingredients:

- 0.5 lb. kabocha squash puree
- 2 cups vegetable stock
- ½ cup chopped onion
- Fresh ground salt and pepper – to taste
- 1 tsp. dried thyme
- 6 oz. broccoli florets
- ½ Tbsp. olive oil
- 1 anise star

MMMMMMMMMMMMMMMMMMMMMMMMMMMMMM

Instructions:

1. Heat olive oil in medium pot and add onion add broccoli, carrots and sauté for 15 minutes, until onion is caramelized.

2. Add thyme and stir well.

3. Transfer the vegetables in a blender, add kabocha squash puree, vegetable stock and pulse until smooth.

4. Transfer the mixture into sauce pan and simmer, add anise star and simmer over medium-high heat for 5-8 minutes or until heated through.

5. Remove the anise star and serve while still hot.

(21) Kabocha Chocolate Chip Muffins

If you are a fan of a kabocha squash and chocolate chips then you will love these muffins.

Makes: 12 muffins

Preparation Time: 35 minutes

List of Ingredients:

- 1 cup cooked and cubed kabocha squash
- 2 tsp. baking soda
- 4 Tbsp. milk
- 1 tsp. allspice
- 1 tsp. cinnamon
- 1 ¾ cups all-purpose flour
- 2 eggs
- 4 Tbsp. vegetable oil
- ¾ cup sugar
- ½ cup chocolate chips, chopped
- 1 pinch salt

MMMMMMMMMMMMMMMMMMMMMMMMMMMMM

Instructions:

1. Preheat oven to 350F and line 12-hole muffin tin with paper cases.

2. In a bowl combine the flour, cinnamon, allspice and baking soda.

3. In a blender process the kabocha squash, milk, oil, eggs and sugar until smooth.

4. Fold the kabocha squash mix into the dry ingredients and stir until just combined. Stir in the chocolate chips and spoon the batter into paper cases to 2/3 full.

5. Bake the muffins for 25 minutes or until firm to the touch. Remove from the oven and allow cooling for 10 minutes. Remove from the tin and serve.

(22) Ginger Spiced Soup

This delicious soup is easy to make and makes for a delicious appetizer.

Makes: 4

Preparation Time: 40 minutes

List of Ingredients:

- 3 red bell peppers, diced
- 1 ½ Tbsp. grass-fed butter
- 2 carrots, grated
- 1 brown onion, diced
- 2 garlic cloves, minced
- 1 ½ Tbsp. tomato puree
- 2 tsp. fresh grated ginger
- 1 tsp. smoked paprika
- 1 bay leaf
- ½ cup chilled coconut cream whisked with 1 Tbsp. lemon juice
- 4 cups home-made vegetable stock
- ½ tsp. ground coriander

MMMMMMMMMMMMMMMMMMMMMMMMMMMMMM

Instructions:

1. Melt butter in medium heavy-bottom pan, over medium-high heat.

2. Add carrots, bell peppers and onion. Cook for 13-15 minutes or until onion is golden, stirring occasionally.

3. Add garlic, ginger, smoked paprika, tomato puree and coriander.

4. Cook until very fragrant, for 2 minutes.

5. Add bay leaf and stock bring to boil and reduce heat to medium-low and simmer for 20-25 minutes.

6. Remove bay leaf and when cooled puree in batches using blender. Process until smooth.

7. Stir in the whisked cream and cook for 10 minutes more or until heated through.

8. Serve while still hot.

(23) White Chocolate Fudge

This fudge requires minimum effort and time to prepare.

Makes: 6

Preparation Time: 10 minutes + inactive time

List of Ingredients:

- 1 Tbsp. coconut butter
- ¾ cup walnuts
- 2 dates, pitted
- 1/3 cup white chocolate chips
- 3 Tbsp. coconut oil
- ¾ cup pecan nuts

MMMMMMMMMMMMMMMMMMMMMMMMMMMMM

Instructions:

1. Add all ingredient to a blender.

2. Process until you have a thick consistency.

3. Line a baking dish with parchment paper and spread the prepared mix in the prepare dish.

4. Cover with foil and refrigerate for 2 hours.

5. Slice and serve.

(24) Kale - Artichoke Dip

Here is a simple recipe that can be a time saver for your next party or movie night.

Makes: 6

Preparation Time: 30 minutes

List of Ingredients:

- ½ cup sour cream
- ½ cup mayonnaise
- 10oz. kale, thawed, drained
- ½ cup artichokes, can, drained
- 1 lemon slice, peeled
- ¼ cup Parmesan, grated
- 1 garlic clove, peeled
- 1 pinch salt
- 1 pinch pepper

MMMMMMMMMMMMMMMMMMMMMMMMMMMMM

Instructions:

1. Preheat oven to 350F.

2. Place all ingredients, except artichoke hearts in a blender.

3. Secure the lid and blend on low for 10 seconds increase speed to medium and blend for 10 seconds more.

4. Add artichokes and secure the lid blend for additional 15 seconds on medium speed. Once blended transfer into oven-safe dish bake the dip for 25 minutes. Serve at room temperature.

(25) Apple Whip

This is very light and delicious dessert you can prepare within few minutes.

Makes: 4

Preparation Time: 10 minutes

List of Ingredients:

- 1 cup coconut milk
- 1 apple, peeled and chopped, frozen overnight

Instructions:

1. Place the ingredients in a blender.

2. Process on high until you have a creamy consistency.

3. Serve immediately.

(26) Tahini Avocado Dip

Now you can use your blender to whip with a delicious dip that can be paired with just about any dip you please.

Makes: 4

Preparation Time: 10 minutes

List of Ingredients:

- 2 Tbsp. parsley, fresh
- 1 lemon, juiced
- 1/3 cup tahini
- 4oz. baby kale
- 1 avocado, pitted, peeled
- ½ tsp. cumin, ground
- 1 pinch salt
- 1 pinch pepper
- ¼ cup water

MMMMMMMMMMMMMMMMMMMMMMMMMMMMMM

Instructions:

1. Heat around 2 Tbsp. water in a skillet over medium-high heat. Add the kale and cook until just wilted.

2. Remove from the heat and drain. Place all ingredients, including kale in a blender. Start blending at the low speed for 10 seconds, Increase the speed gradually and blend on high for 15 seconds more.

3. Add remaining water to thin the dip or even vegetable stock and blend to combine. Serve after.

(27) Strawberry Smoothie

Here is a simple smoothie that is naturally sweet and can be enjoyed as a dessert.

Makes: 1

Preparation Time: 5 minutes

List of Ingredients:

- ½ banana
- 1 cup strawberries, trimmed, frozen
- 1 Tbsp. raw honey
- ¼ tsp. nutmeg
- Almond milk to max line

MMMMMMMMMMMMMMMMMMMMMMMMMMMMMM

Instructions:

1. Place all ingredients in blender.

2. Add enough almond milk to reach the max line.

3. Process ingredients until smooth, for 20 seconds.

4. Serve immediately.

(28) Grapefruit, Banana & Pomegranate Smoothie

Brighten up your day with this simply delicious smoothie.

Makes: 2

Preparation Time: 5 minutes

List of Ingredients:

- 2 segmented Grapefruits
- Pomegranate Juice (1 cup, fresh)
- Banana (½, frozen)
- ½ cup crushed ice
- 1 cup plain yogurt
- 2 Tbsp. honey

MMMMMMMMMMMMMMMMMMMMMMMMMMMMMM

Instructions:

1. Combine all ingredients in blender.

2. Process for 30 seconds or until smooth.

3. Serve immediately in tall glass.

(29) Blackberry Chocolate Blast

This refreshing smoothie is easy to make and delicious.

Makes: 1

Preparation Time: 5 minutes

List of Ingredients:

- 1 cup blackberries
- 1 dash stevia powder
- 1 Tbsp. chocolate chunks
- 1 Tbsp. Chia seeds
- 1 dash cinnamon
- Almond milk to max line

MMMMMMMMMMMMMMMMMMMMMMMMMMMMMM

Instructions:

1. Place blackberries, chocolate chunks, Chia seeds and cinnamon in blender.

2. Add enough almond milk to reach the max line.

3. Process for 30 seconds or until you get smooth mixture.

4. Serve immediately in chilled tall glass.

(30) Roasted Beet Dip

Use your blender to process your roasted beets to create a healthy and delicious dip that pairs well with salted crackers.

Makes: 6

Preparation Time: 1 hour 10 minutes

List of Ingredients:

- 4 cups beet, cut into chunks
- 1 tsp. cumin seeds
- 1 tsp. coriander seeds
- 2 Tbsp. lemon juice
- 3 tsp. garlic, chopped
- 2 Tbsp. extra-virgin olive oil
- 1/3 cup cilantro leaves, fresh, chopped
- 5 tsp. serrano chili, finely chopped
- 1 tsp. salt

MMMMMMMMMMMMMMMMMMMMMMMMMMMMMMM

Instructions:

1. Preheat oven to 400F and prepare rimmed baking sheet.

2. Toss the beets with some olive oil and a pinch of salt. Spread over baking sheet in a single layer and roast for 1 hour or until tender.

3. Once roasted place the beets in a blender.

4. Add remaining ingredients, except cilantro and secure the lid. Set the blender on low and blend for 20 seconds increase the speed to high and blend on high for 30 seconds or until smooth.

5. Transfer in a bowl and stir in cilantro. Serve after.

About the Author

A native of Indianapolis, Indiana, Valeria Ray found her passion for cooking while she was studying English Literature at Oakland City University. She decided to try a cooking course with her friends and the experience changed her forever. She enrolled at the Art Institute of Indiana which offered extensive courses in the culinary Arts. Once Ray dipped her toe in the cooking world, she never looked back.

When Valeria graduated, she worked in French restaurants in the Indianapolis area until she became the head chef at one of the 5-star establishments in the area. Valeria's attention to taste and visual detail caught the eye of a local business person who expressed an interest in publishing her recipes. Valeria began her secondary career authoring cookbooks and e-books which she tackled with as much talent and gusto as her first career. Her passion for food leaps off the page of her books which have colourful anecdotes and stunning pictures of dishes she has prepared herself.

Valeria Ray lives in Indianapolis with her husband of 15 years, Tom, her daughter, Isobel and their loveable Golden Retriever, Goldy. Valeria enjoys cooking special dishes in her large, comfortable kitchen where the family gets involved in preparing meals. This successful, dynamic chef is an inspiration to culinary students and novice cooks everywhere.

Author's Afterthoughts

Thank you for Purchasing my book and taking the time to read it from front to back. I am always grateful when a reader chooses my work and I hope you enjoyed it!

With the vast selection available online, I am touched that you chose to be purchasing my work and take valuable time out of your life to read it. My hope is that you feel you made the right decision.

I very much would like to know what you thought of the book. Please take the time to write an honest and informative review on Amazon.com. Your experience and opinions will be of great benefit to me and those readers looking to make an informed choice.

With much thanks,

Valeria Ray

Made in the USA
Monee, IL
03 December 2020